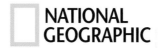
NATIONAL
GEOGRAPHIC

T0045498

We Use Water

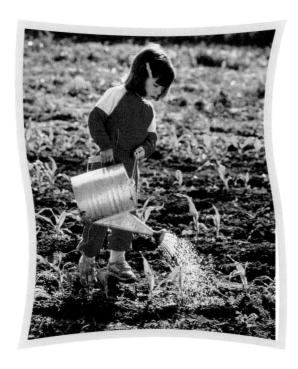

Nick Bruce

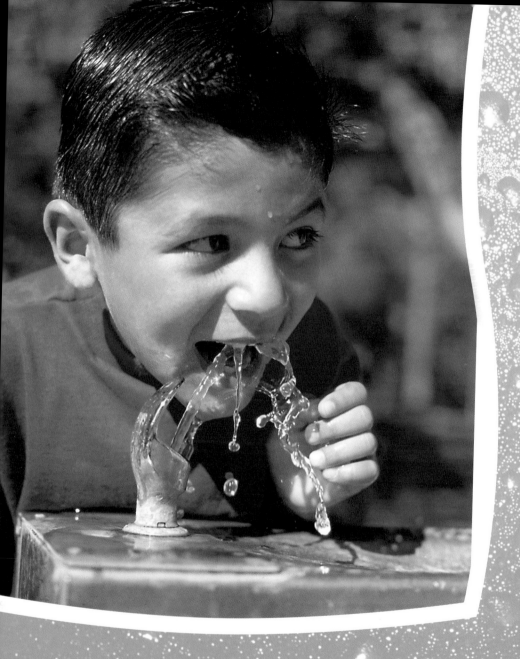

We use water to drink.

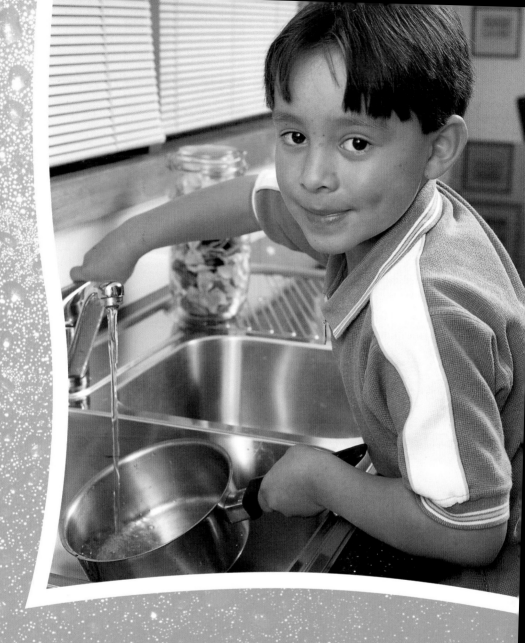

We use water to cook.

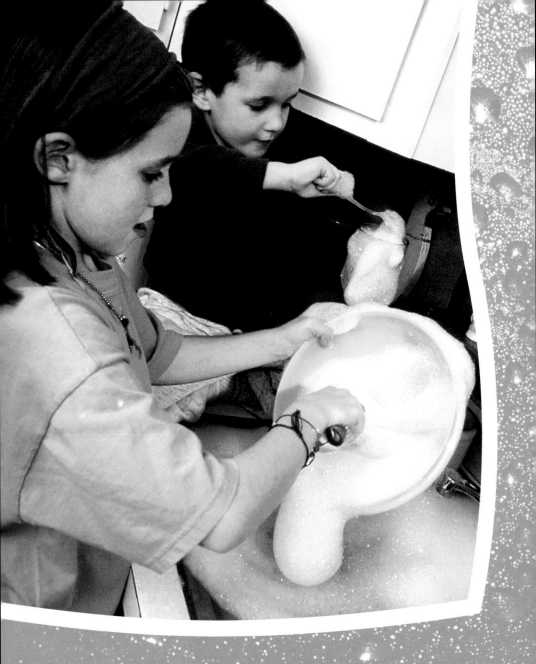

We use water to wash the dishes.

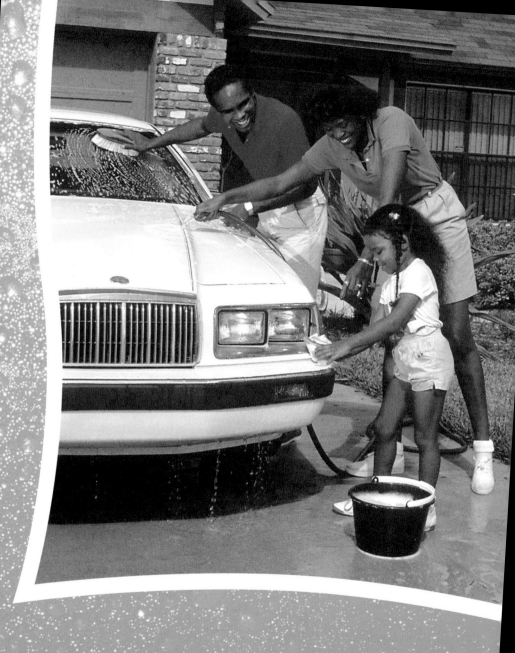

We use water to wash our car.

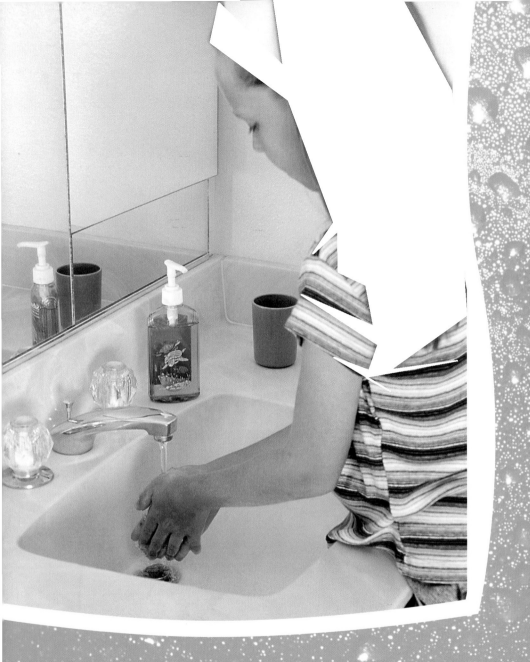

We use water to wash our hands.

6

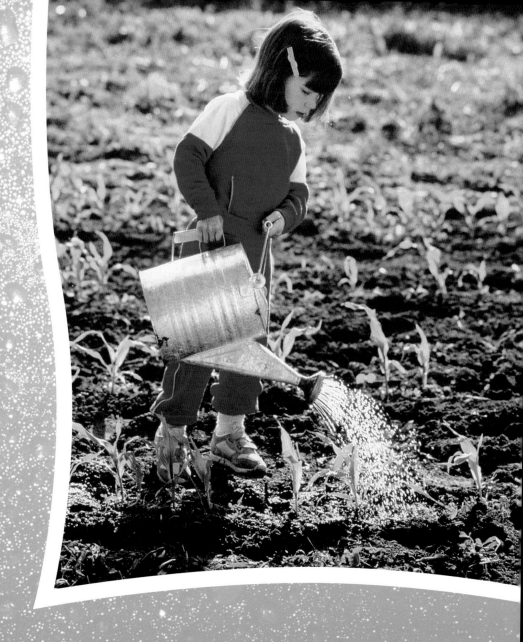

We use water to grow plants.

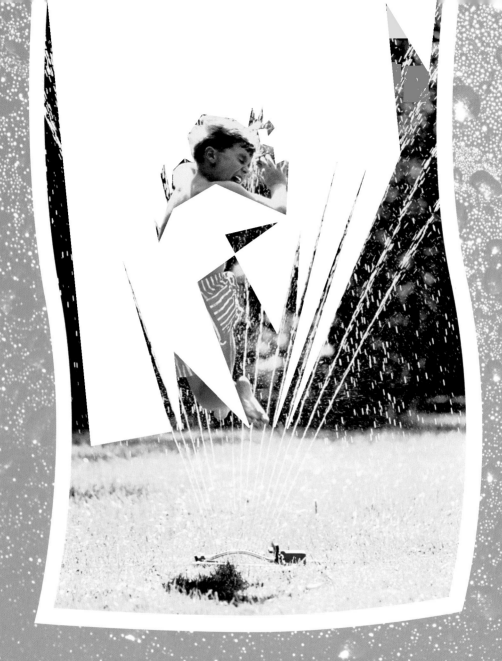

We use water to play.